MY FRIEND WON'T TALK TO ME

TO ME

WORKING IT OUT

You Choose the Ending

by Connie Colwell Miller • illustrated by Sofia Cardoso

Do you ever wish you could change a story or choose a different ending?

IN THESE BOOKS, YOU CAN!

Read along and when you see this:

WHAT HAPPENS NEXT?

Skip to the page for that choice, and see what happens.

In this story, Joey's best friend Presley won't speak to him. Will Joey give his friend space, or will he make things worse? YOU make the choices!

During math, Mr. Leonard calls on Presley for an answer.

"Four?" Presley guesses. The answer is eight.

"I can't believe you didn't know that!" Joey says loudly.

The whole class hears him. Presley is embarrassed and angry.

TURN THE PAGE →

After school, Presley is still mad about Joey's comment in math. Joey wants to play with her, but she is too upset to talk to him.

"I'm sorry, Presley," Joey says. "I didn't mean to embarrass you. Can you forgive me?"

Presley just keeps walking.

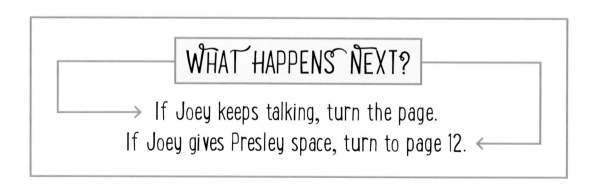

WHAT HAPPENS NEXT?

If Joey keeps talking, turn the page.
If Joey gives Presley space, turn to page 12.

Joey is surprised, and a little mad, that Presley won't speak to him. He thinks she should accept his apology right now.

He keeps asking. "Can't you just get over it, Presley?" Presley keeps walking. She doesn't even look at him.

WHAT HAPPENS NEXT?

→ If Joey keeps pestering, turn the page.

If Joey lets Presley cool down, turn to page 16. ←

"Wow, you're really making a big deal out of this," Joey says. "It wasn't even that mean."

Presley's face burns red.

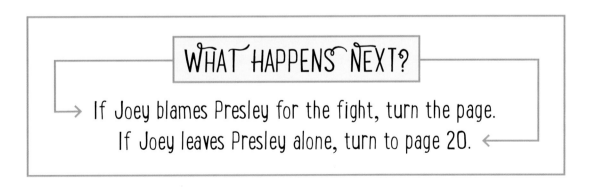

WHAT HAPPENS NEXT?

If Joey blames Presley for the fight, turn the page.

If Joey leaves Presley alone, turn to page 20.

"You're being a huge baby," Joey accuses.

Presley snaps. "I don't want to play with you today or ever again!"

Presley storms home. Joey thinks about what he said and wishes he could take it back. He hopes Presley will forgive him soon. It definitely won't be today.

THE END

→ Go to page 23. ←

"I really am sorry, Presley," Joey says. "But I can see you need time to yourself. Come over to my house if you want to play."

Presley walks home without a word.

TURN THE PAGE →

Presley knows Joey didn't mean to hurt her feelings, but she's still mad. After a few hours, she cools down and feels better.

Presley heads over to Joey's house after dinner. Joey is glad he gave his friend the space she needed.

THE END
Go to page 23.

Presley's eyes look angry. Joey realizes that she needs time. He doesn't understand why she is so mad, but he knows that he can't change her mind right now.

He is a little sad, but he also knows that time can fix things.

TURN THE PAGE →

After dinner, Presley calls. "Hi, Joey, I'm sorry I stopped talking to you. Next time, don't make fun of me in front of the whole class!"

"I understand, Presley. I'm sorry, and I won't do it again. Want to play tomorrow?"

"Sure," she says. "You're still my friend."

Joey is happy they made up and excited for tomorrow.

THE END

Go to page 23.

Joey doesn't understand why Presley is so angry.
But he can tell that he is making the problem worse.
"I'm sorry, Presley. I'll leave you alone."

TURN THE PAGE →

The next day at school, Presley is still mad. Joey wants to talk, but he can tell that Presley isn't ready. Joey realizes that he should give her time.

THE END

THINK AGAIN

- What happened at the end of the path you chose?
- Did you like that ending?
- Go back to page 3. Read the story again and pick different choices. How did the story change?

We all can choose how to act when people aren't speaking to us. If your friend wasn't talking to you because of something you did, would YOU force them to talk, or would you give them space?

For my sweet Irene—C.C.M.

AMICUS ILLUSTRATED is published by Amicus
P.O. Box 227, Mankato, MN 56002
www.amicuspublishing.us

Library of Congress Cataloging-in-Publication Data
Names: Miller, Connie Colwell, 1976- author. | Cardoso, Sofia
   (Illustrator), illustrator.
Title: My friend won't talk to me : working it out : you choose the ending
   / by Connie Colwell Miller ; illustrated by Sofia Cardoso.
Description: Mankato, MN : Amicus. [2023] | Series: Making good choices |
   Audience: Ages 6-9 | Audience: Grades 2-3 | Summary: "In this choose-your-
own-ending picture book, Joey makes fun of his friend Presley in front of the
whole math class. Presley gets so angry that she won't talk to him. Will she
accept his apology and save their friendship? Readers make choices for Joey,
with each story path leading to different outcomes. Includes four endings and
discussion questions"—Provided by publisher.
Identifiers: LCCN 2021056817 (print) | LCCN 2021056818 (ebook) | ISBN
   9781645492771 (hardcover) | ISBN 9781681528014 (paperback) | ISBN
   9781645493655 (ebook)
Subjects: LCSH: Apologizing--Juvenile literature. | Anger in
   children--Juvenile literature. | Friendship in children--Juvenile
   literature.
Classification: LCC BF575.A75 M55 2023 (print) | LCC BF575.A75 (ebook) |
   DDC 302.34083--dc23/eng/20211217
LC record available at https://lccn.loc.gov/2021056817
LC ebook record available at https://lccn.loc.gov/2021056818

Editor: Rebecca Glaser
Series Designer: Kathleen Petelinsek
Book Designer: Catherine Berthiaume

ABOUT THE AUTHOR

Connie Colwell Miller is a writer, editor, and instructor who lives in Le Sueur, Minnesota, with her four children. She has written over 100 books for young children. She likes to tell stories to her kids to teach them important life lessons.

ABOUT THE ILLUSTRATOR

Sofia Cardoso is a Portuguese children's book illustrator, designer, and foodie, whose passion for illustration goes all the way back to her childhood years. Using a mix of both traditional and digital methods, she now spends her days creating whimsical illustrations, full of color and young characters that aim to inspire joy and creativity in both kids and kids at heart.